C000216345

Inspiration

WORDSWORTH

Lakeland Poetry

Publisher and Creative Director: Nick Wells
Project Editor: Gillian Whitaker
Art Director: Mike Spender
Layout Design: Jane Ashley
Digital Design and Production: Chris Herbert

FLAME TREE PUBLISHING

6 Melbray Mews
London SW6 3NS
United Kingdom

www.flametreepublishing.com

First published 2020

20 21 22 23 24
1 2 3 4 5 6 7 8 9 10

A CIP record for this book is available from the British Library upon request.

ISBN 978-1-83964-162-6

Printed in China | Created, Developed & Produced in the United Kingdom

Inspiration

WORDSWORTH

Lakeland Poetry

Introduction by
Sally Bushell

FLAME TREE
PUBLISHING

CONTENTS

Introduction
6

Nature & The Sublime
10

Childhood & Memory
52

Solitude & Loss
88

Society & Daily Life
134

Index
158

INTRODUCTION

William Wordsworth lived through turbulent times; he was a young man in his twenties when the French Revolution re-determined European politics in the late eighteenth Century. Wordsworth experienced the Revolution at first hand, travelling across France in a walking tour in 1790, and returning there in 1791–92. 'Bliss was it in that dawn to be alive, But to be young was very heaven!' he declared in his autobiographic epic, *The Prelude*. The democratic principles of natural freedoms that underpinned the Revolution were soon to find literary expression in British Romanticism. Poets turned away from high generic forms to embrace a much wider range of poetry including song, and ballad – forms of the ordinary man on the street. Right at the heart of this movement, and spokesperson for it in his Preface to *Lyrical Ballads* (1800), was Wordsworth. The nature, subject and language of poetry were all radically redefined by him in the light of these revolutionary principles. Poetry was no longer a polite conversation between the elite, but about individual self-expression: 'all good poetry is the spontaneous overflow of powerful feelings' (1800 Preface). From this perspective, the Poet is 'a man, speaking to men' whose role it is to 'chuse incidents and situations from common life, and to relate or describe them, throughout, as far as was possible, in a selection of language really used by men' (1802 Preface). Although these principles seem obvious to us today, these were controversial ideas for the time that heralded the British Romantic movement in literature.

In December 1799, William, and his sister Dorothy, rented Dove Cottage in Town End, Grasmere and, in so doing, returned home to Cumberland and Westmorland and set up house together for the first time. They had both been born in Cockermouth in the North of the Lake District: William on April 7th 1770 with Dorothy the next child born next after him (on Christmas Day, 1771), the second and third of five children. Wordsworth's father, John, was law-agent for James Lowther, Earl of Lonsdale, so that the family lived rent-free in an imposing house in the centre of town. In 1778, Wordsworth's mother, Ann, died, followed in 1783 by the death of their father, and the family was split up. The four boys stayed with their mother's family in Penrith and were sent to Hawkshead Grammar school but Dorothy, as the only girl, was sent to live with her mother's cousin in Halifax, Yorkshire.

Early experiences of adventures around Hawkshead and the Vale of Esthwaite during this time proved crucial to the adult poet.

In Book XI of his autobiographical epic *The Prelude* Wordsworth defined such childhood experiences as universal 'spots of time' – early memories suspended in our minds, but vital to our identities and to the adults that we later become.

When he left school, Wordsworth went on to Cambridge (which he did not enjoy) then, in 1796, met fellow-poet Samuel Taylor Coleridge who was to be a key influence on his life and writing. The Wordsworths and Coleridge lived as neighbours for a while in Somerset – where their joint collection, *Lyrical Ballads* was planned. After a brief stay in Germany, the Wordsworths returned to England and finally chose to settle in the Lake District (with Coleridge moving up soon after to live close by). This was a significant decision for an ambitious young poet. Wordsworth deliberately situated himself remotely, in the country, at a considerable distance from the fashionable metropolis. He wanted to write about the lives of those around him and show that their stories were capable of being as powerful and moving as that of any gentleman in London.

A powerful sense of place is therefore central to all of Wordsworth's poetic output. William's decision to live in Grasmere led to him writing poems about the local region and its inhabitants, and even to write in the landscape itself (he often chose to write outdoors, pacing up and down in the woods). Poems like 'Michael' are suffused with a sense of loss and sadness that perhaps relates to Wordsworth himself. Although he has returned home, he is also profoundly aware that he can never inhabit place in the instinctive ways of the shepherd for whom 'these fields, these hills … were his living Being, even more / Than his own Blood'. But Wordsworth also writes for future generations, for 'youthful Poets, who … will be my second self when I am gone'. The creation of the National Trust and of the Lake District National Park, by Victorian admirers of Wordsworth's poetry, makes it possible for this wish to come true.

Sally Bushell

Sally Bushell is Professor of Romantic and Victorian Literature and co-director of The Wordsworth Centre at Lancaster University (on the edge of the Lake District). She has a long-standing research interest in Wordsworth's poetry and his representation of the layered meanings of place, space and region. She is also editor of the *Cambridge Companion to Lyrical Ballads* (2019).

NATURE
&
THE SUBLIME

An Evening Walk (extracts)

Bright'ning the cliffs between, where sombrous pine
And yew-trees o'er the silver rocks recline;
I love to mark the quarry's moving trains,
Dwarf panniered steeds, and men, and numerous wains:
How busy the enormous hive within,
While Echo dallies with the various din!
Some (hardly heard their chisel's clinking sound)
Toil, small as pigmies, in the gulf profound;
Some, dim between th' aereal cliffs descry'd,
O'erwalk the slender plank from side to side;
These, by the pale-blue rocks that ceaseless ring,
Glad from their airy baskets hang and sing.

* *

Now, while the solemn evening Shadows sail
On red slow-waving pinions down the vale,
How pleasant near the tranquil lake to stray,
Where winds the road along a secret bay;
By rills that tumble down the woody steeps,
And run in transport to the dimpling deeps;
Along the 'wild meandering shore' to view,

Obsequious Grace the winding swan pursue.
He swells his lifted chest, and backward flings
His bridling neck between his towering wings;
In all the majesty of ease divides,
And glorying looks around, the silent tides:
On as he floats, the silvered waters glow,
Proud of the varying arch and moveless form of snow.
While tender Cares and mild domestic Loves
With furtive watch pursue her as she moves;
The Female with a meeker charm succeeds,
And her brown Little-ones around her leads,
Nibbling the water-lilies as they pass,
Or playing wanton with the floating grass.
She, in a mother's care, her beauty's pride
Forgets, unweary'd watching every side:
She calls them near, and with affection sweet
Alternately relieves their weary feet;
Alternately they mount her back, and rest,
Close by her mantling wings' embraces prest.

* *

Now with religious awe the farewell light
Blends with the solemn colouring of the night;

Mid groves of clouds that crest the mountain's brow,
And round the West's proud lodge their shadows throw,
Like Una shining on her gloomy way,
The half-seen form of Twilight roams astray;
Shedding, through paly loopholes mild and small,
Gleams that upon the lake's still bosom fall,
Beyond the mountain's giant reach that hides
In deep determined gloom his subject tides.
Soft o'er the surface creep those lustres pale
Tracking the fitful motions of the gale.
With restless interchange at once the bright
Wins on the shade, the shade upon the light.
No favoured eye was e'er allowed to gaze
On lovelier spectacle in faery days;
When gentle Spirits urged a sportive chase,
Brushing with lucid wands the water's face;
While music, stealing round the glimmering deeps,
Charmed the tall circle of th' enchanted steeps.
—The lights are vanished from the watery plains:
No wreck of all the pageantry remains.
Unheeded Night has overcome the vales:
On the dark earth the baffled vision fails;
The latest lingerer of the forest train,
The lone black fir, forsakes the faded plain;

Last evening sight, the cottage smoke no more,
Lost in the thickened darkness, glimmers hoar;
And, towering from the sullen dark-brown mere,
Like a black wall, the mountain steeps appear.
—Now o'er the soothed accordant heart we feel
A sympathetic twilight slowly steal,
And ever, as we fondly muse, we find
The soft gloom deepening on the tranquil mind.
Stay! pensive, sadly-pleasing visions, stay!
Ah no! as fades the vale, they fade away.
Yet still the tender, vacant gloom remains;
Still the cold cheek its shuddering tear retains.

The bird, who ceased, with fading light, to thread
Silent the hedge or steaming rivulet's bed,
From his grey re-appearing tower shall soon
Salute with boding note the rising moon,
Frosting with hoary light the pearly ground,
And pouring deeper blue to Aether's bound;
And pleased her solemn pomp of clouds to fold
In robes of azure, fleecy-white, and gold.
See, o'er the eastern hill, where Darkness broods
O'er all its vanished dells, and lawns, and woods;
Where but a mass of shade the sight can trace,

She lifts in silence up her lovely face;
Above the gloomy valley flings her light,
Far to the western slopes with hamlets white;
And gives, where woods the chequered upland strew,
To the green corn of summer autumn's hue.
Thus Hope, first pouring from her blessed horn
Her dawn, far lovelier than the Moon's own morn;
'Till higher mounted, strives in vain to cheer
The weary hills, impervious, blackening near;
—Yet does she still, undaunted, throw the while
On darling spots remote her tempting smile.
—Ev'n now she decks for me a distant scene,
(For dark and broad the gulph of time between)
Gilding that cottage with her fondest ray,
(Sole bourn, sole wish, sole object of my way;
How fair its lawns and sheltering woods appear!
How sweet its streamlet murmurs in mine ear!)
Where we, my friend, to happy days shall rise,
'Till our small share of hardly-paining sighs
(For sighs will ever trouble human breath)
Creep hushed into the tranquil breast of Death.

1787–89

A Night Piece

—The sky is overcast
With a continuous cloud of texture close,
Heavy and wan, all whitened by the Moon,
Which through that veil is indistinctly seen,
A dull, contracted circle, yielding light
So feebly spread, that not a shadow falls,
Chequering the ground – from rock, plant, tree, or tower.
At length a pleasant instantaneous gleam
Startles the pensive traveller while he treads
His lonesome path, with unobserving eye
Bent earthwards; he looks up – the clouds are split
Asunder, – and above his head he sees
The clear Moon, and the glory of the heavens.
There, in a black-blue vault she sails along,
Followed by multitudes of stars, that, small
And sharp, and bright, along the dark abyss
Drive as she drives: how fast they wheel away,
Yet vanish not! – the wind is in the tree,
But they are silent; – still they roll along
Immeasurably distant; and the vault,
Built round by those white clouds, enormous clouds,

Still deepens its unfathomable depth.
At length the Vision closes; and the mind,
Not undisturbed by the delight it feels,
Which slowly settles into peaceful calm,
Is left to muse upon the solemn scene.

1798

A Whirl-blast from Behind the Hill

A whirl-blast from behind the hill
Rush'd o'er the wood with startling sound:
Then all at once the air was still,
And showers of hail-stones patter'd round.
Where leafless Oaks tower'd high above,
I sate within an undergrove
Of tallest hollies, tall and green,
A fairer bower was never seen.
From year to year the spacious floor
With wither'd leaves is cover'd o'er,
You could not lay a hair between:
And all the year the bower is green.
But see! where'er the hailstones drop
The wither'd leaves all skip and hop,
There's not a breeze – no breath of air—
Yet here, and there, and every where
Along the floor, beneath the shade
By those embowering hollies made,
The leaves in myriads jump and spring,

As if with pipes and music rare
Some Robin Good-fellow were there,
And all those leaves, that jump and spring,
Were each a joyous, living thing.

Oh! grant me Heaven a heart at ease
That I may never cease to find,
Even in appearances like these
Enough to nourish and to stir my mind!

1798

LINES WRITTEN IN EARLY SPRING

I heard a thousand blended notes,
While in a grove I sate reclined,
In that sweet mood when pleasant thoughts
Bring sad thoughts to the mind.

To her fair works did Nature link
The human soul that through me ran;
And much it grieved my heart to think
What man has made of man.

Through primrose tufts, in that green bower,
The periwinkle trailed its wreaths;
And 'tis my faith that every flower
Enjoys the air it breathes.

The birds around me hopped and played,
Their thoughts I cannot measure—
But the least motion which they made,
It seemed a thrill of pleasure.

The budding twigs spread out their fan,
To catch the breezy air;
And I must think, do all I can,
That there was pleasure there.

If this belief from heaven be sent,
If such be Nature's holy plan,
Have I not reason to lament
What man has made of man?

1798

Expostulation and Reply

'Why, William, on that old grey stone,
Thus for the length of half a day,
Why, William, sit you thus alone,
And dream your time away?

'Where are your books? – that light bequeathed
To Beings else forlorn and blind!
Up! Up! and drink the spirit breathed
From dead men to their kind.

'You look round on your Mother Earth,
As if she for no purpose bore you;
As if you were her first-born birth,
And none had lived before you!'

One morning thus, by Esthwaite lake,
When life was sweet, I knew not why,
To me my good friend Matthew spake,
And thus I made reply.

'The eye – it cannot choose but see;
We cannot bid the ear be still;
Our bodies feel, where'er they be,
Against or with our will.

'Nor less I deem that there are Powers
Which of themselves our minds impress;
That we can feed this mind of ours
In a wise passiveness.

'Think you, 'mid all this mighty sum
Of things for ever speaking,
That nothing of itself will come,
But we must still be seeking?

' —Then ask not wherefore, here, alone,
Conversing as I may,
I sit upon this old grey stone,
And dream my time away.'

1798

THE TABLES TURNED

An Evening Scene on the Same Subject

Up! Up! my Friend, and quit your books;
Or surely you'll grow double:
Up! Up! my Friend, and clear your looks;
Why all this toil and trouble?

The sun, above the mountain's head,
A freshening lustre mellow
Through all the long green fields has spread,
His first sweet evening yellow.

Books! 'tis a dull and endless strife:
Come, hear the woodland linnet,
How sweet his music! on my life,
There's more of wisdom in it.

And hark! how blithe the throstle sings!
He, too, is no mean preacher:
Come forth into the light of things,
Let Nature be your Teacher.

She has a world of ready wealth,
Our minds and hearts to bless—
Spontaneous wisdom breathed by health,
Truth breathed by cheerfulness.

One impulse from a vernal wood
May teach you more of man,
Of moral evil and of good,
Than all the sages can.

Sweet is the lore which Nature brings;
Our meddling intellect
Mis-shapes the beauteous forms of things:
—We murder to dissect.

Enough of Science and of Art;
Close up those barren leaves;
Come forth, and bring with you a heart
That watches and receives.

1798

Hart-Leap Well

Part the First

The Knight had ridden down from Wensley Moor
With the slow motion of a summer's cloud
And now, as he approached a vassal's door,
'Bring forth another horse!' he cried aloud.

'Another horse!' – That shout the vassal heard
And saddled his best Steed, a comely grey;
Sir Walter mounted him; he was the third
Which he had mounted on that glorious day.

Joy sparkled in the prancing courser's eyes;
The horse and horseman are a happy pair;
But, though Sir Walter like a falcon flies,
There is a doleful silence in the air.

A rout this morning left Sir Walter's Hall,
That as they galloped made the echoes roar;
But horse and man are vanished, one and all;
Such race, I think, was never seen before.

Sir Walter, restless as a veering wind,
Calls to the few tired dogs that yet remain:
Blanch, Swift, and Music, noblest of their kind,
Follow, and up the weary mountain strain.

The Knight hallooed, he cheered and chid them on
With suppliant gestures and upbraidings stern;
But breath and eyesight fail; and, one by one,
The dogs are stretched among the mountain fern.

Where is the throng, the tumult of the race?
The bugles that so joyfully were blown?
—This chase it looks not like an earthly chase;
Sir Walter and the Hart are left alone.

The poor Hart toils along the mountain-side;
I will not stop to tell how far he fled,
Nor will I mention by what death he died;
But now the Knight beholds him lying dead.

Dismounting, then, he leaned against a thorn;
He had no follower, dog, nor man, nor boy:
He neither cracked his whip, nor blew his horn,
But gazed upon the spoil with silent joy.

Close to the thorn on which Sir Walter leaned,
Stood his dumb partner in this glorious feat;
Weak as a lamb the hour that it is yeaned;
And white with foam as if with cleaving sleet.

Upon his side the Hart was lying stretched:
His nostril touched a spring beneath a hill,
And with the last deep groan his breath had fetched
The waters of the spring were trembling still.

And now, too happy for repose or rest,
(Never had living man such joyful lot!)
Sir Walter walked all round, north, south, and west,
And gazed and gazed upon that darling spot.

And climbing up the hill – (it was at least
Four roods of sheer ascent) Sir Walter found
Three several hoof-marks which the hunted Beast
Had left imprinted on the grassy ground.

Sir Walter wiped his face, and cried, 'Till now
Such sight was never seen by human eyes:
Three leaps have borne him from this lofty brow,
Down to the very fountain where he lies.

'I'll build a pleasure-house upon this spot,
And a small arbour, made for rural joy;
'Twill be the traveller's shed, the pilgrim's cot,
A place of love for damsels that are coy.

'A cunning artist will I have to frame
A basin for that fountain in the dell!
And they who do make mention of the same,
From this day forth, shall call it Hart-Leap Well.

'And, gallant Stag! to make thy praises known,
Another monument shall here be raised;
Three several pillars, each a rough-hewn stone,
And planted where thy hoofs the turf have grazed.

'And, in the summer-time when days are long,
I will come hither with my Paramour;
And with the dancers and the minstrel's song
We will make merry in that pleasant bower.

'Till the foundations of the mountains fail
My mansion with its arbour shall endure;
—The joy of them who till the fields of Swale,
And them who dwell among the woods of Ure!'

Then home he went, and left the Hart, stone-dead,
With breathless nostrils stretched above the spring.
—Soon did the Knight perform what he had said;
And far and wide the fame thereof did ring.

Ere thrice the Moon into her port had steered,
A cup of stone received the living well;
Three pillars of rude stone Sir Walter reared,
And built a house of pleasure in the dell.

And near the fountain, flowers of stature tall
With trailing plants and trees were intertwined,
—Which soon composed a little sylvan hall,
A leafy shelter from the sun and wind.

And thither, when the summer days were long
Sir Walter led his wondering Paramour;
And with the dancers and the minstrel's song
Made merriment within that pleasant bower.

The Knight, Sir Walter, died in course of time,
And his bones lie in his paternal vale.
—But there is matter for a second rhyme,
And I to this would add another tale.

Part the Second

The moving accident is not my trade;
To freeze the blood I have no ready arts:
'Tis my delight, alone in summer shade,
To pipe a simple song for thinking hearts.

As I from Hawes to Richmond did repair,
It chanced that I saw standing in a dell
Three aspens at three corners of a square;
And one, not four yards distant, near a well.

What this imported I could ill divine:
And, pulling now the rein my horse to stop,
I saw three pillars standing in a line,
—The last stone-pillar on a dark hill-top.

The trees were grey, with neither arms nor head:
Half wasted the square mound of tawny green;
So that you just might say, as then I said,
'Here in old time the hand of man hath been.'

I looked upon the hill both far and near,
More doleful place did never eye survey;
It seemed as if the spring-time came not here,
And Nature here were willing to decay.

I stood in various thoughts and fancies lost,
When one, who was in shepherd's garb attired,
Came up the hollow: – him did I accost,
And what this place might be I then inquired.

The Shepherd stopped, and that same story told
Which in my former rhyme I have rehearsed.
'A jolly place,' said he, 'in times of old!
But something ails it now: the spot is curst.

'You see these lifeless stumps of aspen wood—
Some say that they are beeches, others elms—
These were the bower; and here a mansion stood,
The finest palace of a hundred realms!

'The arbour does its own condition tell;
You see the stones, the fountain, and the stream;
But as to the great Lodge! you might as well
Hunt half a day for a forgotten dream.

'There's neither dog nor heifer, horse nor sheep,
Will wet his lips within that cup of stone;
And oftentimes, when all are fast asleep,
This water doth send forth a dolorous groan.

'Some say that here a murder has been done,
And blood cries out for blood: but, for my part,
I've guessed, when I've been sitting in the sun,
That it was all for that unhappy Hart.

'What thoughts must through the creature's brain have past!
Even from the topmost stone, upon the steep,
Are but three bounds – and look, Sir, at this last—
O Master! it has been a cruel leap.

'For thirteen hours he ran a desperate race;
And in my simple mind we cannot tell
What cause the Hart might have to love this place,
And come and make his death-bed near the well.

'Here on the grass perhaps asleep he sank,
Lulled by the fountain in the summer tide;
This water was perhaps the first he drank
When he had wandered from his mother's side.

'In April here beneath the flowering thorn
He heard the birds their morning carols sing;
And he, perhaps, for aught we know, was born
Not half a furlong from that self-same spring.

'Now, here is neither grass nor pleasant shade;
The sun on drearier hollow never shone;
So will it be, as I have often said,
Till trees, and stones, and fountain, all are gone.'

'Grey-headed Shepherd, thou hast spoken well;
Small difference lies between thy creed and mine:
This Beast not unobserved by Nature fell;
His death was mourned by sympathy divine.

'The Being, that is in the clouds and air,
That is in the green leaves among the groves,
Maintains a deep and reverential care
For the unoffending creatures whom he loves.

'The pleasure-house is dust: – behind, before,
This is no common waste, no common gloom;
But Nature, in due course of time, once more
Shall here put on her beauty and her bloom.

'She leaves these objects to a slow decay,
That what we are, and have been, may be known;
But at the coming of the milder day,
These monuments shall all be overgrown.

'One lesson, Shepherd, let us two divide,
Taught both by what she shows, and what conceals;
Never to blend our pleasure or our pride
With sorrow of the meanest thing that feels.'

1800

It Was an April Morning: Fresh and Clear

It was an April morning: fresh and clear
The Rivulet, delighting in its strength,
Ran with a young man's speed; and yet the voice
Of waters which the winter had supplied
Was softened down into a vernal tone.
The spirit of enjoyment and desire,
And hopes and wishes, from all living things
Went circling, like a multitude of sounds.
The budding groves seemed eager to urge on
The steps of June; as if their various hues
Were only hindrances that stood between
Them and their object: but, meanwhile, prevailed
Such an entire contentment in the air
That every naked ash, and tardy tree
Yet leafless, showed as if the countenance
With which it looked on this delightful day
Were native to the summer. – Up the brook
I roamed in the confusion of my heart,
Alive to all things and forgetting all.
At length I to a sudden turning came
In this continuous glen, where down a rock

The Stream, so ardent in its course before,
Sent forth such sallies of glad sound, that all
Which I till then had heard, appeared the voice
Of common pleasure: beast and bird, the lamb,
The shepherd's dog, the linnet and the thrush
Vied with this waterfall, and made a song,
Which, while I listened, seemed like the wild growth
Or like some natural produce of the air,
That could not cease to be. Green leaves were here;
But 'twas the foliage of the rocks – the birch,
The yew, the holly, and the bright green thorn,
With hanging islands of resplendent furze:
And, on a summit, distant a short space,
By any who should look beyond the dell,
A single mountain-cottage might be seen.
I gazed and gazed, and to myself I said,
'Our thoughts at least are ours; and this wild nook,
My Emma, I will dedicate to thee.'
—Soon did the spot become my other home,
My dwelling, and my out-of-doors abode.
And, of the Shepherds who have seen me there,

To whom I sometimes in our idle talk
Have told this fancy, two or three, perhaps,
Years after we are gone and in our graves,
When they have cause to speak of this wild place,
May call it by the name of Emma's Dell.

c. 1800

ON NATURE'S INVITATION DO I COME

On Nature's invitation do I come,
By Reason sanctioned. Can the choice mislead,
That made the calmest, fairest spot of earth,
With all its unappropriated good,
My own, and not mine only, for with me
Entrenched – say rather peacefully embowered—
Under yon orchard, in yon humble cot,
A younger orphan of a home extinct,
The only daughter of my parents dwells:
Aye, think on that, my heart, and cease to stir;
Pause upon that, and let the breathing frame
No longer breathe, but all be satisfied.
Oh, if such silence be not thanks to God
For what hath been bestowed, then where, where then
Shall gratitude find rest? Mine eyes did ne'er
Fix on a lovely object, nor my mind
Take pleasure in the midst of happy thoughts,
But either she, whom now I have, who now
Divides with me this loved abode, was there,
Or not far off. Where'er my footsteps turned,
Her voice was like a hidden bird that sang;
The thought of her was like a flash of light

Or an unseen companionship, a breath
Or fragrance independent of the wind.
In all my goings, in the new and old
Of all my meditations, and in this
Favourite of all, in this the most of all…
Embrace me then, ye hills, and close me in.
Now in the clear and open day I feel
Your guardianship: I take it to my heart;
'Tis like the solemn shelter of the night.
But I would call thee beautiful; for mild,
And soft, and gay, and beautiful thou art,
Dear valley, having in thy face a smile,
Though peaceful, full of gladness. Thou art pleased,
Pleased with thy crags, and woody steeps, thy lake,
Its one green island, and its winding shores,
The multitude of little rocky hills,
Thy church, and cottages of mountain-stone
Clustered like stars some few, but single most,
And lurking dimly in their shy retreats,
Or glancing at each other cheerful looks,
Like separated stars with clouds between.

c. 1800

My Heart Leaps up when I Behold

My heart leaps up when I behold
A rainbow in the sky:
So was it when my life began;
So is it now I am a man;
So be it when I shall grow old,
Or let me die!
The Child is father of the Man;
And I could wish my days to be
Bound each to each by natural piety.

1802

It is a Beauteous Evening, Calm and Free

It is a beauteous evening, calm and free,
The holy time is quiet as a Nun
Breathless with adoration; the broad sun
Is sinking down in its tranquillity;
The gentleness of heaven broods o'er the Sea:
Listen! the mighty Being is awake,
And doth with his eternal motion make
A sound like thunder – everlastingly.
Dear Child! dear Girl! that walkest with me here,
If thou appear untouched by solemn thought,
Thy nature is not therefore less divine:
Thou liest in Abraham's bosom all the year;
And worshipp'st at the Temple's inner shrine,
God being with thee when we know it not.

1802

COMPOSED UPON WESTMINSTER BRIDGE, SEPTEMBER 3, 1802

Earth has not any thing to show more fair:
Dull would he be of soul who could pass by
A sight so touching in its majesty:
This City now doth, like a garment, wear
The beauty of the morning; silent, bare,
Ships, towers, domes, theatres, and temples lie
Open unto the fields, and to the sky;
All bright and glittering in the smokeless air.
Never did sun more beautifully steep
In his first splendour, valley, rock, or hill;
Ne'er saw I, never felt, a calm so deep!
The river glideth at his own sweet will:
Dear God! the very houses seem asleep;
And all that mighty heart is lying still!

1802

SHE WAS A PHANTOM OF DELIGHT

She was a Phantom of delight
When first she gleamed upon my sight;
A lovely Apparition, sent
To be a moment's ornament;
Her eyes as stars of Twilight fair;
Like Twilight's, too, her dusky hair;
But all things else about her drawn
From May-time and the cheerful Dawn;
A dancing Shape, an Image gay,
To haunt, to startle, and way-lay.

I saw her upon nearer view,
A Spirit, yet a Woman too!
Her household motions light and free,
And steps of virgin-liberty;
A countenance in which did meet
Sweet records, promises as sweet;
A Creature not too bright or good
For human nature's daily food;
For transient sorrows, simple wiles,
Praise, blame, love, kisses, tears, and smiles.

And now I see with eye serene
The very pulse of the machine;
A Being breathing thoughtful breath,
A Traveller between life and death;
The reason firm, the temperate will,
Endurance, foresight, strength, and skill;
A perfect Woman, nobly planned,
To warn, to comfort, and command;
And yet a Spirit still, and bright
With something of angelic light.

1804

To a Sky-Lark

Up with me! up with me into the clouds!
For thy song, Lark, is strong;
Up with me, up with me into the clouds!
Singing, singing,
With clouds and sky about thee ringing,
Lift me, guide me till I find
That spot which seems so to thy mind!

I have walked through wildernesses dreary,
And today my heart is weary;
Had I now the wings of a Faery,
Up to thee would I fly.
There is madness about thee, and joy divine
In that song of thine;
Lift me, guide me high and high
To thy banqueting-place in the sky.

Joyous as morning,
Thou art laughing and scorning;
Thou hast a nest for thy love and thy rest,
And, though little troubled with sloth,

Drunken Lark! thou would'st be loth
To be such a traveller as I.
Happy, happy Liver,
With a soul as strong as a mountain river
Pouring out praise to the almighty Giver,
Joy and jollity be with us both!

Alas! my journey, rugged and uneven,
Through prickly moors or dusty ways must wind;
But hearing thee, or others of thy kind,
As full of gladness and as free of heaven,
I, with my fate contented, will plod on,
And hope for higher raptures, when life's day is done.

1805

Oh Nightingale, Thou Surely Art

O Nightingale! thou surely art
A creature of a 'fiery heart'—
These notes of thine – they pierce and pierce;
Tumultuous harmony and fierce!
Thou sing'st as if the God of wine
Had helped thee to a Valentine;
A song in mockery and despite
Of shades, and dews, and silent night;
And steady bliss, and all the loves
Now sleeping in these peaceful groves.

I heard a Stock-dove sing or say
His homely tale, this very day;
His voice was buried among trees,
Yet to be come-at by the breeze:
He did not cease; but cooed – and cooed;

And somewhat pensively he wooed:
He sang of love, with quiet blending,
Slow to begin, and never ending;
Of serious faith, and inward glee;
That was the song – the song for me!

1807

THE FAIREST, BRIGHTEST HUES OF ETHER FADE

The fairest, brightest, hues of ether fade;
The sweetest notes must terminate and die;
O Friend! thy flute has breathed a harmony
Softly resounded through this rocky glade;
Such strains of rapture as the Genius played
In his still haunt on Bagdad's summit high;
He who stood visible to Mirza's eye,
Never before to human sight betrayed.
Lo, in the vale, the mists of evening spread!
The visionary Arches are not there,
Nor the green Islands, nor the shining Seas;
Yet sacred is to me this Mountain's head,
Whence I have risen, uplifted on the breeze
Of harmony, above all earthly care.

published 1815

The Stars Are Mansions Built by Nature's Hand

The stars are mansions built by Nature's hand,
And, haply, there the spirits of the blest
Dwell, clothed in radiance, their immortal vest;
Huge Ocean shows, within his yellow strand,
A habitation marvellously planned,
For life to occupy in love and rest;
All that we see – is dome, or vault, or nest,
Or fortress, reared at Nature's sage command.
Glad thought for every season! but the Spring
Gave it while cares were weighing on my heart,
'Mid song of birds, and insects murmuring;
And while the youthful year's prolific art—
Of bud, leaf, blade, and flower – was fashioning
Abodes where self-disturbance hath no part.

1820

CHILDHOOD

&

MEMORY

THE PRELUDE (BOOK I) (EXTRACT)

One summer evening (led by her) I found
A little boat tied to a willow tree
Within a rocky cave, its usual home.
Straight I unloosed her chain, and stepping in
Pushed from the shore. It was an act of stealth
And troubled pleasure, nor without the voice
Of mountain-echoes did my boat move on;
Leaving behind her still, on either side,
Small circles glittering idly in the moon,
Until they melted all into one track
Of sparkling light. But now, like one who rows,
Proud of his skill, to reach a chosen point
With an unswerving line, I fixed my view
Upon the summit of a craggy ridge,
The horizon's utmost boundary; far above
Was nothing but the stars and the grey sky.
She was an elfin pinnace; lustily
I dipped my oars into the silent lake,
And, as I rose upon the stroke, my boat
Went heaving through the water like a swan;
When, from behind that craggy steep till then
The horizon's bound, a huge peak, black and huge,

As if with voluntary power instinct
Upreared its head. I struck and struck again,
And growing still in stature the grim shape
Towered up between me and the stars, and still,
For so it seemed, with purpose of its own
And measured motion like a living thing,
Strode after me. With trembling oars I turned,
And through the silent water stole my way
Back to the covert of the willow tree;
There in her mooring-place I left my bark,—
And through the meadows homeward went, in grave
And serious mood; but after I had seen
That spectacle, for many days, my brain
Worked with a dim and undetermined sense
Of unknown modes of being; o'er my thoughts
There hung a darkness, call it solitude
Or blank desertion. No familiar shapes
Remained, no pleasant images of trees,
Of sea or sky, no colours of green fields;
But huge and mighty forms, that do not live
Like living men, moved slowly through the mind
By day, and were a trouble to my dreams.

    Wisdom and Spirit of the universe!
Thou Soul that art the eternity of thought,

That givest to forms and images a breath
And everlasting motion, not in vain
By day or star-light thus from my first dawn
Of childhood didst thou intertwine for me
The passions that build up our human soul;
Not with the mean and vulgar works of man,
But with high objects, with enduring things—
With life and nature, purifying thus
The elements of feeling and of thought,
And sanctifying, by such discipline,
Both pain and fear, until we recognise
A grandeur in the beatings of the heart.

    Nor was this fellowship vouchsafed to me
With stinted kindness. In November days,
When vapours rolling down the valley made
A lonely scene more lonesome, among woods
At noon, and 'mid the calm of summer nights,
When, by the margin of the trembling lake,
Beneath the gloomy hills homeward I went
In solitude, such intercourse was mine;
Mine was it in the fields both day and night,
And by the waters, all the summer long.

1798–1839

ANECDOTE FOR FATHERS

I have a boy of five years old;
His face is fair and fresh to see;
His limbs are cast in beauty's mould,
And dearly he loves me.

One morn we strolled on our dry walk,
Our quiet home all full in view,
And held such intermitted talk
As we are wont to do.

My thoughts on former pleasures ran;
I thought of Kilve's delightful shore,
Our pleasant home when spring began,
A long, long year before.

A day it was when I could bear
Some fond regrets to entertain;
With so much happiness to spare,
I could not feel a pain.

The green earth echoed to the feet
Of lambs that bounded through the glade,
From shade to sunshine, and as fleet
From sunshine back to shade.

Birds warbled round me – and each trace
Of inward sadness had its charm;
Kilve, thought I, was a favoured place,
And so is Liswyn farm.

My boy beside me tripped, so slim
And graceful in his rustic dress!
And, as we talked, I questioned him,
In very idleness.

'Now tell me, had you rather be,'
I said, and took him by the arm,
'On Kilve's smooth shore, by the green sea,
Or here at Liswyn farm?'

In careless mood he looked at me,
While still I held him by the arm,
And said, 'At Kilve I'd rather be
Than here at Liswyn farm.'

'Now, little Edward, say why so:
My little Edward, tell me why.'
—'I cannot tell, I do not know.'
—'Why, this is strange,' said I;

'For, here are woods, hills smooth and warm:
There surely must some reason be
Why you would change sweet Liswyn farm
For Kilve by the green sea.'

At this, my boy hung down his head,
He blushed with shame, nor made reply;
And three times to the child I said,
'Why, Edward, tell me why?'

His head he raised – there was in sight,
It caught his eye, he saw it plain—
Upon the house-top, glittering bright,
A broad and gilded vane.

Then did the boy his tongue unlock,
And eased his mind with this reply:
'At Kilve there was no weather-cock;
And that's the reason why.'

O dearest, dearest boy! my heart
For better lore would seldom yearn,
Could I but teach the hundredth part
Of what from thee I learn.

1798

Lines, Composed a Few Miles Above Tintern Abbey

Five years have past; five summers, with the length
Of five long winters! and again I hear
These waters, rolling from their mountain-springs
With a soft inland murmur. – Once again
Do I behold these steep and lofty cliffs,
That on a wild secluded scene impress
Thoughts of more deep seclusion; and connect
The landscape with the quiet of the sky.
The day is come when I again repose
Here, under this dark sycamore, and view
These plots of cottage-ground, these orchard-tufts,
Which at this season, with their unripe fruits,
Are clad in one green hue, and lose themselves
'Mid groves and copses. Once again I see
These hedge-rows, hardly hedge-rows, little lines
Of sportive wood run wild: these pastoral farms,
Green to the very door; and wreaths of smoke
Sent up, in silence, from among the trees!
With some uncertain notice, as might seem
Of vagrant dwellers in the houseless woods,
Or of some Hermit's cave, where by his fire
The Hermit sits alone.

These beauteous forms,
Through a long absence, have not been to me
As is a landscape to a blind man's eye:
But oft, in lonely rooms, and 'mid the din
Of towns and cities, I have owed to them,
In hours of weariness, sensations sweet,
Felt in the blood, and felt along the heart;
And passing even into my purer mind,
With tranquil restoration: – feelings too
Of unremembered pleasure: such, perhaps,
As have no slight or trivial influence
On that best portion of a good man's life,
His little, nameless, unremembered, acts
Of kindness and of love. Nor less, I trust,
To them I may have owed another gift,
Of aspect more sublime; that blessed mood,
In which the burthen of the mystery,
In which the heavy and the weary weight
Of all this unintelligible world,
Is lightened: – that serene and blessed mood,
In which the affections gently lead us on,
—Until, the breath of this corporeal frame

And even the motion of our human blood
Almost suspended, we are laid asleep
In body, and become a living soul:
While with an eye made quiet by the power
Of harmony, and the deep power of joy,
We see into the life of things.

    If this
Be but a vain belief, yet, oh! how oft—
In darkness and amid the many shapes
Of joyless daylight; when the fretful stir
Unprofitable, and the fever of the world,
Have hung upon the beatings of my heart—
How oft, in spirit, have I turned to thee,
O sylvan Wye! thou wanderer thro' the woods,
How often has my spirit turned to thee!

And now, with gleams of half-extinguished thought,
With many recognitions dim and faint,
And somewhat of a sad perplexity,
The picture of the mind revives again:
While here I stand, not only with the sense
Of present pleasure, but with pleasing thoughts
That in this moment there is life and food

For future years. And so I dare to hope,
Though changed, no doubt, from what I was when first
I came among these hills; when like a roe
I bounded o'er the mountains, by the sides
Of the deep rivers, and the lonely streams,
Wherever nature led: more like a man
Flying from something that he dreads, than one
Who sought the thing he loved. For nature then
(The coarser pleasures of my boyish days,
And their glad animal movements all gone by)
To me was all in all. – I cannot paint
What then I was. The sounding cataract
Haunted me like a passion: the tall rock,
The mountain, and the deep and gloomy wood,
Their colours and their forms, were then to me
An appetite; a feeling and a love,
That had no need of a remoter charm,
By thought supplied, nor any interest
Unborrowed from the eye. – That time is past,
And all its aching joys are now no more,
And all its dizzy raptures. Not for this
Faint I, nor mourn nor murmur; other gifts
Have followed; for such loss, I would believe,
Abundant recompence. For I have learned

To look on nature, not as in the hour
Of thoughtless youth; but hearing oftentimes
The still, sad music of humanity,
Nor harsh nor grating, though of ample power
To chasten and subdue. And I have felt
A presence that disturbs me with the joy
Of elevated thoughts; a sense sublime
Of something far more deeply interfused,
Whose dwelling is the light of setting suns,
And the round ocean and the living air,
And the blue sky, and in the mind of man:
A motion and a spirit, that impels
All thinking things, all objects of all thought,
And rolls through all things. Therefore am I still
A lover of the meadows and the woods,
And mountains; and of all that we behold
From this green earth; of all the mighty world
Of eye, and ear, – both what they half create,
And what perceive; well pleased to recognise
In nature and the language of the sense,
The anchor of my purest thoughts, the nurse,
The guide, the guardian of my heart, and soul
Of all my moral being.

    Nor perchance,
If I were not thus taught, should I the more
Suffer my genial spirits to decay:
For thou art with me here upon the banks
Of this fair river; thou my dearest Friend,
My dear, dear Friend; and in thy voice I catch
The language of my former heart, and read
My former pleasures in the shooting lights
Of thy wild eyes, Oh! yet a little while
May I behold in thee what I was once,
My dear, dear Sister! and this prayer I make,
Knowing that Nature never did betray
The heart that loved her; 'tis her privilege,
Through all the years of this our life, to lead
From joy to joy: for she can so inform
The mind that is within us, so impress
With quietness and beauty, and so feed
With lofty thoughts, that neither evil tongues,
Rash judgments, nor the sneers of selfish men,
Nor greetings where no kindness is, nor all
The dreary intercourse of daily life,
Shall e'er prevail against us, or disturb
Our cheerful faith, that all which we behold

Is full of blessings. Therefore let the moon

Shine on thee in thy solitary walk;

And let the misty mountain-winds be free

To blow against thee: and, in after years,

When these wild ecstasies shall be matured

Into a sober pleasure; when thy mind

Shall be a mansion for all lovely forms,

Thy memory be as a dwelling-place

For all sweet sounds and harmonies; oh! then,

If solitude, or fear, or pain, or grief,

Should be thy portion, with what healing thoughts

Of tender joy wilt thou remember me,

And these my exhortations! Nor, perchance—

If I should be where I no more can hear

Thy voice, nor catch from thy wild eyes these gleams

Of past existence – wilt thou then forget

That on the banks of this delightful stream

We stood together; and that I, so long

A worshipper of Nature, hither came

Unwearied in that service: rather say

With warmer love – oh! with far deeper zeal

Of holier love. Nor wilt thou then forget,

That after many wanderings, many years

Of absence, these steep woods and lofty cliffs,
And this green pastoral landscape, were to me
More dear, both for themselves and for thy sake!

1798

THE FOUNTAIN

A Conversation

We talked with open heart, and tongue
Affectionate and true,
A pair of friends, though I was young,
And Matthew seventy-two.

We lay beneath a spreading oak,
Beside a mossy seat;
And from the turf a fountain broke,
And gurgled at our feet.

'Now, Matthew!' said I, 'let us match
This water's pleasant tune
With some old border-song, or catch
That suits a summer's noon;

'Or of the church-clock and the chimes
Sing here beneath the shade,
That half-mad thing of witty rhymes
Which you last April made!'

In silence Matthew lay, and eyed
The spring beneath the tree;
And thus the dear old Man replied,
The grey-haired man of glee:

'No check, no stay, this Streamlet fears;
How merrily it goes!
'Twill murmur on a thousand years,
And flow as now it flows.

'And here, on this delightful day,
I cannot choose but think
How oft, a vigorous man, I lay
Beside this fountain's brink.

'My eyes are dim with childish tears,
My heart is idly stirred,
For the same sound is in my ears
Which in those days I heard.

'Thus fares it still in our decay:
And yet the wiser mind
Mourns less for what age takes away
Than what it leaves behind.

'The blackbird amid leafy trees,
The lark above the hill,
Let loose their carols when they please,
Are quiet when they will.

'With Nature never do they wage
A foolish strife; they see
A happy youth, and their old age
Is beautiful and free:

'But we are pressed by heavy laws;
And often, glad no more,
We wear a face of joy, because
We have been glad of yore.

'If there be one who need bemoan
His kindred laid in earth,
The household hearts that were his own;
It is the man of mirth.

'My days, my Friend, are almost gone,
My life has been approved,
And many love me; but by none
Am I enough beloved.'

'Now both himself and me he wrongs,
The man who thus complains!
I live and sing my idle songs
Upon these happy plains;

'And, Matthew, for thy children dead
I'll be a son to thee!'
At this he grasped my hand, and said,
'Alas! that cannot be.'

We rose up from the fountain-side;
And down the smooth descent
Of the green sheep-track did we glide;
And through the wood we went;

And, ere we came to Leonard's rock,
He sang those witty rhymes
About the crazy old church-clock,
And the bewildered chimes.

1799

THE SPARROW'S NEST

Behold, within the leafy shade,
Those bright blue eggs together laid!
On me the chance-discovered sight
Gleamed like a vision of delight.
I started – seeming to espy
The home and sheltered bed,
The Sparrow's dwelling, which, hard by
My Father's house, in wet or dry
My sister Emmeline and I
Together visited.
She looked at it and seemed to fear it;
Dreading, tho' wishing, to be near it:
Such heart was in her, being then
A little Prattler among men.
The Blessing of my later years
Was with me when a boy:
She gave me eyes, she gave me ears;
And humble cares, and delicate fears;
A heart, the fountain of sweet tears;
And love, and thought, and joy.

1801

TO A BUTTERFLY

Stay near me – do not take thy flight!
A little longer stay in sight!
Much converse do I find in thee,
Historian of my infancy!
Float near me; do not yet depart!
Dead times revive in thee:
Thou bring'st, gay creature as thou art!
A solemn image to my heart,
My father's family!

Oh! pleasant, pleasant were the days,
The time, when, in our childish plays,
My sister Emmeline and I
Together chased the butterfly!
A very hunter did I rush
Upon the prey: – with leaps and springs
I followed on from brake to bush;
But she, God love her! feared to brush
The dust from off its wings.

1802

ODE: INTIMATIONS OF IMMORTALITY FROM RECOLLECTIONS OF EARLY CHILDHOOD

There was a time when meadow, grove, and stream,
The earth, and every common sight,
To me did seem
Apparelled in celestial light,
The glory and the freshness of a dream.
It is not now as it hath been of yore;—
Turn wheresoe'er I may,
By night or day,
The things which I have seen I now can see no more.

The Rainbow comes and goes,
And lovely is the Rose,
The Moon doth with delight
Look round her when the heavens are bare,
Waters on a starry night
Are beautiful and fair;
The sunshine is a glorious birth;
But yet I know, where'er I go,
That there hath passed away a glory from the earth.

Now, while the birds thus sing a joyous song,

And while the young lambs bound

As to the tabor's sound,

To me alone there came a thought of grief:

A timely utterance gave that thought relief,

And I again am strong:

The cataracts blow their trumpets from the steep;

No more shall grief of mine the season wrong;

I hear the Echoes through the mountains throng,

The Winds come to me from the fields of sleep,

And all the earth is gay;

Land and sea

Give themselves up to jollity,

And with the heart of May

Doth every Beast keep holiday;—

Thou Child of Joy,

Shout round me, let me hear thy shouts, thou happy

Shepherd-boy!

Ye blessed Creatures, I have heard the call

Ye to each other make; I see

The heavens laugh with you in your jubilee;

My heart is at your festival,

My head hath its coronal,

The fulness of your bliss, I feel – I feel it all.

Oh evil day! if I were sullen

While Earth herself is adorning,

This sweet May-morning,

And the Children are culling

On every side,

In a thousand valleys far and wide,

Fresh flowers; while the sun shines warm,

And the Babe leaps up on his Mother's arm:—

I hear, I hear, with joy I hear!

—But there's a Tree, of many, one,

A single Field which I have looked upon,

Both of them speak of something that is gone:

The Pansy at my feet

Doth the same tale repeat:

Whither is fled the visionary gleam?

Where is it now, the glory and the dream?

Our birth is but a sleep and a forgetting:
The Soul that rises with us, our life's Star,
Hath had elsewhere its setting,
And cometh from afar:
Not in entire forgetfulness,
And not in utter nakedness,
But trailing clouds of glory do we come
From God, who is our home:
Heaven lies about us in our infancy!
Shades of the prison-house begin to close
Upon the growing Boy,
But He beholds the light, and whence it flows
He sees it in his joy;
The Youth, who daily farther from the east
Must travel, still is Nature's Priest,
And by the vision splendid
Is on his way attended;
At length the Man perceives it die away,
And fade into the light of common day.

Earth fills her lap with pleasures of her own;
Yearnings she hath in her own natural kind,
And, even with something of a Mother's mind,

And no unworthy aim,
The homely Nurse doth all she can
To make her Foster-child, her Inmate Man,
Forget the glories he hath known,
And that imperial palace whence he came.

Behold the Child among his new-born blisses,
A six years' Darling of a pigmy size!
See, where 'mid work of his own hand he lies,
Fretted by sallies of his mother's kisses,
With light upon him from his father's eyes!
See, at his feet, some little plan or chart,
Some fragment from his dream of human life,
Shaped by himself with newly-learned art;
A wedding or a festival,
A mourning or a funeral;
And this hath now his heart,
And unto this he frames his song:
Then will he fit his tongue
To dialogues of business, love, or strife;
But it will not be long
Ere this be thrown aside,
And with new joy and pride

The little Actor cons another part;
Filling from time to time his 'humorous stage'
With all the Persons, down to palsied Age,
That Life brings with her in her equipage;
As if his whole vocation
Were endless imitation.

Thou, whose exterior semblance doth belie
Thy Soul's immensity;
Thou best Philosopher, who yet dost keep
Thy heritage, thou Eye among the blind,
That, deaf and silent, read'st the eternal deep,
Haunted for ever by the eternal mind,
—Mighty Prophet! Seer blest!
On whom those truths do rest,
Which we are toiling all our lives to find,
In darkness lost, the darkness of the grave;
Thou, over whom thy Immortality
Broods like the Day, a Master o'er a Slave,
A Presence which is not to be put by;
Thou little Child, yet glorious in the might
Of heaven-born freedom on thy being's height,
Why with such earnest pains dost thou provoke

The years to bring the inevitable yoke,
Thus blindly with thy blessedness at strife?
Full soon thy Soul shall have her earthly freight,
And custom lie upon thee with a weight,
Heavy as frost, and deep almost as life!

O joy! that in our embers
Is something that doth live,
That nature yet remembers
What was so fugitive!
The thought of our past years in me doth breed
Perpetual benediction; not indeed
For that which is most worthy to be blest;
Delight and liberty, the simple creed
Of Childhood, whether busy or at rest,
With new-fledged hope still fluttering in his breast:—
Not for these I raise
The song of thanks and praise;
But for those obstinate questionings
Of sense and outward things,
Fallings from us, vanishings;
Blank misgivings of a Creature
Moving about in worlds not realised,

High instincts before which our mortal Nature
Did tremble like a guilty Thing surprised:
But for those first affections,
Those shadowy recollections,
Which, be they what they may,
Are yet the fountain light of all our day,
Are yet a master light of all our seeing;
Uphold us, cherish, and have power to make
Our noisy years seem moments in the being
Of the eternal Silence: truths that wake,
To perish never;

Which neither listlessness, nor mad endeavour,
Nor Man nor Boy,
Nor all that is at enmity with joy,
Can utterly abolish or destroy!
Hence in a season of calm weather,
Though inland far we be,
Our Souls have sight of that immortal sea
Which brought us hither,
Can in a moment travel thither,
And see the Children sport upon the shore,
And hear the mighty waters rolling evermore.

Then sing, ye Birds, sing, sing a joyous song!

And let the young Lambs bound

As to the tabor's sound!

We in thought will join your throng,

Ye that pipe and ye that play,

Ye that through your hearts today

Feel the gladness of the May!

What though the radiance which was once so bright

Be now for ever taken from my sight,

Though nothing can bring back the hour

Of splendour in the grass, of glory in the flower;

We will grieve not, rather find

Strength in what remains behind;

In the primal sympathy

Which having been must ever be;

In the soothing thoughts that spring

Out of human suffering;

In the faith that looks through death,

In years that bring the philosophic mind.

And O, ye Fountains, Meadows, Hills, and Groves,

Forebode not any severing of our loves!

Yet in my heart of hearts I feel your might;

I only have relinquished one delight
To live beneath your more habitual sway.
I love the Brooks which down their channels fret,
Even more than when I tripped lightly as they;
The innocent brightness of a new-born Day
Is lovely yet;
The Clouds that gather round the setting sun
Do take a sober colouring from an eye
That hath kept watch o'er man's mortality;
Another race hath been, and other palms are won.
Thanks to the human heart by which we live,
Thanks to its tenderness, its joys, and fears,
To me the meanest flower that blows can give
Thoughts that do often lie too deep for tears.

1803–06

I Wandered Lonely as a Cloud

I wandered lonely as a cloud
That floats on high o'er vales and hills,
When all at once I saw a crowd,
A host, of golden daffodils;
Beside the lake, beneath the trees,
Fluttering and dancing in the breeze.

Continuous as the stars that shine
And twinkle on the milky way,
They stretched in never-ending line
Along the margin of a bay:
Ten thousand saw I at a glance,
Tossing their heads in sprightly dance.

The waves beside them danced; but they
Out-did the sparkling waves in glee:
A poet could not but be gay,
In such a jocund company:
I gazed – and gazed – but little thought
What wealth the show to me had brought:

For oft, when on my couch I lie
In vacant or in pensive mood,
They flash upon that inward eye
Which is the bliss of solitude;
And then my heart with pleasure fills,
And dances with the daffodils.

1804

THERE IS A LITTLE UNPRETENDING RILL

There is a little unpretending Rill
Of limpid water, humbler far than aught
That ever among Men or Naiads sought
Notice or name! – It quivers down the hill,
Furrowing its shallow way with dubious will;
Yet to my mind this scanty Stream is brought
Oftener than Ganges or the Nile; a thought
Of private recollection sweet and still!
Months perish with their moons; year treads on year;
But, faithful Emma! thou with me canst say
That, while ten thousand pleasures disappear,
And flies their memory fast almost as they,
The immortal Spirit of one happy day
Lingers beside that Rill, in vision clear.

c. 1806

To the Cuckoo

Not the whole warbling grove in concert heard
When sunshine follows shower, the breast can thrill
Like the first summons, Cuckoo! of thy bill,
With its twin notes inseparably paired.
The captive 'mid damp vaults unsunned, unaired,
Measuring the periods of his lonely doom,
That cry can reach; and to the sick man's room
Sends gladness, by no languid smile declared.
The lordly eagle-race through hostile search
May perish; time may come when never more
The wilderness shall hear the lion roar;
But, long as cock shall crow from household perch
To rouse the dawn, soft gales shall speed thy wing,
And thy erratic voice be faithful to the Spring!

1827

SOLITUDE

&

LOSS

Calm Is All Nature as a Resting Wheel

Calm is all nature as a resting wheel.
The kine are couched upon the dewy grass;
The horse alone, seen dimly as I pass,
Is cropping audibly his later meal:
Dark is the ground; a slumber seems to steal
O'er vale, and mountain, and the starless sky.
Now, in this blank of things, a harmony,
Home-felt, and home-created, comes to heal
That grief for which the senses still supply
Fresh food; for only then, when memory
Is hushed, am I at rest. My Friends! restrain
Those busy cares that would allay my pain;
Oh! leave me to myself, nor let me feel
The officious touch that makes me droop again.

c. 1786

Animal Tranquillity and Decay

The little hedgerow birds,
That peck along the road, regard him not.
He travels on, and in his face, his step,
His gait, is one expression: every limb,
His look and bending figure, all bespeak
A man who does not move with pain, but moves
With thought. – He is insensibly subdued
To settled quiet: he is one by whom
All effort seems forgotten; one to whom
Long patience hath such mild composure given,
That patience now doth seem a thing of which
He hath no need. He is by nature led
To peace so perfect that the young behold
With envy, what the Old Man hardly feels.

1797

WE ARE SEVEN

—A simple Child,
That lightly draws its breath,
And feels its life in every limb,
What should it know of death?

I met a little cottage Girl:
She was eight years old, she said;
Her hair was thick with many a curl
That clustered round her head.

She had a rustic, woodland air,
And she was wildly clad:
Her eyes were fair, and very fair;
—Her beauty made me glad.

'Sisters and brothers, little Maid,
How many may you be?'
'How many? Seven in all,' she said,
And wondering looked at me.

'And where are they? I pray you tell.'
She answered, 'Seven are we;
And two of us at Conway dwell,
And two are gone to sea.

'Two of us in the church-yard lie,
My sister and my brother;
And, in the church-yard cottage, I
Dwell near them with my mother.'

'You say that two at Conway dwell,
And two are gone to sea,
Yet ye are seven! I pray you tell,
Sweet Maid, how this may be.'

Then did the little Maid reply,
'Seven boys and girls are we;
Two of us in the church-yard lie,
Beneath the church-yard tree.'

'You run about, my little Maid,
Your limbs they are alive;
If two are in the church-yard laid,
Then ye are only five.'

'Their graves are green, they may be seen,'
The little Maid replied,
'Twelve steps or more from my mother's door,
And they are side by side.

'My stockings there I often knit,
My kerchief there I hem;
And there upon the ground I sit,
And sing a song to them.

'And often after sunset, Sir,
When it is light and fair,
I take my little porringer,
And eat my supper there.

'The first that died was sister Jane;
In bed she moaning lay,
Till God released her of her pain;
And then she went away.

'So in the church-yard she was laid;
And, when the grass was dry,
Together round her grave we played,
My brother John and I.

'And when the ground was white with snow,
And I could run and slide,
My brother John was forced to go,
And he lies by her side.'

'How many are you, then,' said I,
'If they two are in heaven?'
Quick was the little Maid's reply,
'O Master! we are seven.'

'But they are dead; those two are dead!
Their spirits are in heaven!'
'Twas throwing words away; for still
The little Maid would have her will,
And said, 'Nay, we are seven!'

1798

Matthew

If Nature, for a favourite child,
In thee hath tempered so her clay,
That every hour thy heart runs wild,
Yet never once doth go astray,

Read o'er these lines; and then review
This tablet, that thus humbly rears
In such diversity of hue
Its history of two hundred years.

—When through this little wreck of fame,
Cipher and syllable! thine eye
Has travelled down to Matthew's name,
Pause with no common sympathy.

And; if a sleeping tear should wake,
Then be it neither checked nor stayed:
For Matthew a request I make
Which for himself he had not made.

Poor Matthew, all his frolics o'er,
Is silent as a standing pool;
Far from the chimney's merry roar,
And murmur of the village school.

The sighs which Matthew heaved were sighs
Of one tired out with fun and madness;
The tears which came to Matthew's eyes
Were tears of light, the dew of gladness.

Yet, sometimes, when the secret cup
Of still and serious thought went round,
It seemed as if he drank it up—
He felt with spirit so profound.

—Thou soul of God's best earthly mould!
Thou happy Soul! and can it be
That these two words of glittering gold
Are all that must remain of thee?

1799

A Slumber Did My Spirit Seal

A slumber did my spirit seal;
I had no human fears:
She seemed a thing that could not feel
The touch of earthly years.

No motion has she now, no force;
She neither hears nor sees;
Rolled round in earth's diurnal course,
With rocks, and stones, and trees.

1799

She Dwelt Among the Untrodden Ways

She dwelt among the untrodden ways
Beside the springs of Dove,
A Maid whom there were none to praise
And very few to love:

A violet by a mossy stone
Half hidden from the eye!
—Fair as a star, when only one
Is shining in the sky.

She lived unknown, and few could know
When Lucy ceased to be;
But she is in her grave, and, oh,
The difference to me!

1799

STRANGE FITS OF PASSION HAVE I KNOWN

Strange fits of passion have I known:
And I will dare to tell,
But in the Lover's ear alone,
What once to me befel.

When she I loved looked every day
Fresh as a rose in June,
I to her cottage bent my way,
Beneath an evening moon.

Upon the moon I fixed my eye,
All over the wide lea;
With quickening pace my horse drew nigh
Those paths so dear to me.

And now we reached the orchard-plot;
And, as we climbed the hill,
The sinking moon to Lucy's cot
Came near, and nearer still.

In one of those sweet dreams I slept,
Kind Nature's gentlest boon!
And all the while my eyes I kept
On the descending moon.

My horse moved on; hoof after hoof
He raised, and never stopped:
When down behind the cottage roof,
At once, the bright moon dropped.

What fond and wayward thoughts will slide
Into a Lover's head!
'O mercy!' to myself I cried,
'If Lucy should be dead!'

1799

Lucy Gray; or, Solitude

Oft I had heard of Lucy Gray:
And, when I crossed the wild,
I chanced to see at break of day
The solitary child.

No mate, no comrade Lucy knew;
She dwelt on a wide moor,
—The sweetest thing that ever grew
Beside a human door!

You yet may spy the fawn at play,
The hare upon the green;
But the sweet face of Lucy Gray
Will never more be seen.

'Tonight will be a stormy night—
You to the town must go;
And take a lantern, Child, to light
Your mother through the snow.'

'That, Father! will I gladly do:
'Tis scarcely afternoon—
The minster-clock has just struck two,
And yonder is the moon!'

At this the Father raised his hook,
And snapped a faggot-band;
He plied his work; – and Lucy took
The lantern in her hand.

Not blither is the mountain roe:
With many a wanton stroke
Her feet disperse the powdery snow,
That rises up like smoke.

The storm came on before its time:
She wandered up and down;
And many a hill did Lucy climb
But never reached the town.

The wretched parents all that night
Went shouting far and wide;
But there was neither sound nor sight
To serve them for a guide.

At day-break on a hill they stood
That overlooked the moor;
And thence they saw the bridge of wood,
A furlong from their door.

They wept – and, turning homeward, cried,
'In heaven we all shall meet';
—When in the snow the mother spied
The print of Lucy's feet.

Then downwards from the steep hill's edge
They tracked the footmarks small;
And through the broken hawthorn hedge,
And by the long stone-wall;

And then an open field they crossed:
The marks were still the same;
They tracked them on, nor ever lost;
And to the bridge they came.

They followed from the snowy bank
Those footmarks, one by one,
Into the middle of the plank;
And further there were none!

—Yet some maintain that to this day
She is a living child;
That you may see sweet Lucy Gray
Upon the lonesome wild.

O'er rough and smooth she trips along,
And never looks behind;
And sings a solitary song
That whistles in the wind.

1799

THREE YEARS SHE GREW IN SUN AND SHOWER

Three years she grew in sun and shower,
Then Nature said, 'A lovelier flower
On earth was never sown;
This Child I to myself will take;
She shall be mine, and I will make
A Lady of my own.

'Myself will to my darling be
Both law and impulse: and with me
The Girl, in rock and plain,
In earth and heaven, in glade and bower,
Shall feel an overseeing power
To kindle or restrain.

'She shall be sportive as the fawn
That wild with glee across the lawn
Or up the mountain springs;
And hers shall be the breathing balm,
And hers the silence and the calm
Of mute insensate things.

'The floating clouds their state shall lend
To her; for her the willow bend;
Nor shall she fail to see
Even in the motions of the Storm
Grace that shall mould the Maiden's form
By silent sympathy.

'The stars of midnight shall be dear
To her; and she shall lean her ear
In many a secret place
Where rivulets dance their wayward round,
And beauty born of murmuring sound
Shall pass into her face.

'And vital feelings of delight
Shall rear her form to stately height,
Her virgin bosom swell;
Such thoughts to Lucy I will give
While she and I together live
Here in this happy dell.'

Thus Nature spake – The work was done—
How soon my Lucy's race was run!
She died, and left to me
This heath, this calm, and quiet scene;
The memory of what has been,
And never more will be.

1799

MICHAEL (EXTRACT)

Near the tumultuous brook of Green-head Ghyll,
In that deep valley, Michael had designed
To build a Sheep-fold; and, before he heard
The tidings of his melancholy loss,
For this same purpose he had gathered up
A heap of stones, which by the streamlet's edge
Lay thrown together, ready for the work.
With Luke that evening thitherward he walked:
And soon as they had reached the place he stopped,
And thus the old Man spake to him: – 'My Son,
Tomorrow thou wilt leave me: with full heart
I look upon thee, for thou art the same
That wert a promise to me ere thy birth,
And all thy life hast been my daily joy.
I will relate to thee some little part
Of our two histories; 'twill do thee good
When thou art from me, even if I should touch
On things thou canst not know of. – After thou
First cam'st into the world – as oft befals
To new-born infants – thou didst sleep away
Two days, and blessings from thy Father's tongue
Then fell upon thee. Day by day passed on,

And still I loved thee with increasing love.
Never to living ear came sweeter sounds
Than when I heard thee by our own fireside
First uttering, without words, a natural tune;
While thou, a feeding babe, didst in thy joy
Sing at thy Mother's breast. Month followed month,
And in the open fields my life was passed
And on the mountains; else I think that thou
Hadst been brought up upon thy Father's knees.
But we were playmates, Luke: among these hills,
As well thou knowest, in us the old and young
Have played together, nor with me didst thou
Lack any pleasure which a boy can know.'
Luke had a manly heart; but at these words
He sobbed aloud. The old Man grasped his hand,
And said, 'Nay, do not take it so – I see
That these are things of which I need not speak.
—Even to the utmost I have been to thee
A kind and a good Father: and herein
I but repay a gift which I myself
Received at others' hands; for, though now old
Beyond the common life of man, I still

Remember them who loved me in my youth.
Both of them sleep together: here they lived,
As all their Forefathers had done; and when
At length their time was come, they were not loth
To give their bodies to the family mould.
I wished that thou should'st live the life they lived:
But, 'tis a long time to look back, my Son,
And see so little gain from threescore years.
These fields were burthened when they came to me;
Till I was forty years of age, not more
Than half of my inheritance was mine.
I toiled and toiled; God blessed me in my work,
And till these three weeks past the land was free.
—It looks as if it never could endure
Another Master. Heaven forgive me, Luke,
If I judge ill for thee, but it seems good
That thou should'st go,'
     At this the old Man paused;
Then, pointing to the stones near which they stood,
Thus, after a short silence, he resumed:
'This was a work for us; and now, my Son,
It is a work for me. But, lay one stone—
Here, lay it for me, Luke, with thine own hands.
Nay, Boy, be of good hope; – we both may live

To see a better day. At eighty-four
I still am strong and hale; – do thou thy part;
I will do mine. – I will begin again
With many tasks that were resigned to thee:
Up to the heights, and in among the storms,
Will I without thee go again, and do
All works which I was wont to do alone,
Before I knew thy face. – Heaven bless thee, Boy!
Thy heart these two weeks has been beating fast
With many hopes; it should be so – yes – yes—
I knew that thou could'st never have a wish
To leave me, Luke: thou hast been bound to me
Only by links of love: when thou art gone,
What will be left to us! – But, I forget
My purposes. Lay now the corner-stone,
As I requested; and hereafter, Luke,
When thou art gone away, should evil men
Be thy companions, think of me, my Son,
And of this moment; hither turn thy thoughts,
And God will strengthen thee: amid all fear
And all temptation, Luke, I pray that thou
May'st bear in mind the life thy Fathers lived,
Who, being innocent, did for that cause
Bestir them in good deeds. Now, fare thee well—

When thou return'st, thou in this place wilt see
A work which is not here: a covenant
'Twill be between us; but, whatever fate
Befal thee, I shall love thee to the last,
And bear thy memory with me to the grave.'

   The Shepherd ended here; and Luke stooped down,
And, as his Father had requested, laid
The first stone of the Sheep-fold. At the sight
The old Man's grief broke from him; to his heart
He pressed his Son, he kissed him and wept;
And to the house together they returned.
—Hushed was that House in peace, or seeming peace,
Ere the night fell: – with morrow's dawn the Boy
Began his journey, and when he had reached
The public way, he put on a bold face;
And all the neighbours, as he passed their doors,
Came forth with wishes and with farewell prayers,
That followed him till he was out of sight.

   A good report did from their Kinsman come,
Of Luke and his well doing: and the Boy
Wrote loving letters, full of wondrous news,
Which, as the Housewife phrased it, were throughout
'The prettiest letters that were ever seen.'
Both parents read them with rejoicing hearts.

So, many months passed on: and once again
The Shepherd went about his daily work
With confident and cheerful thoughts; and now
Sometimes when he could find a leisure hour
He to that valley took his way, and there
Wrought at the Sheep-fold. Meantime Luke began
To slacken in his duty; and, at length,
He in the dissolute city gave himself
To evil courses: ignominy and shame
Fell on him, so that he was driven at last
To seek a hiding-place beyond the seas.

    There is a comfort in the strength of love;
'Twill make a thing endurable, which else
Would overset the brain, or break the heart:
I have conversed with more than one who well
Remember the old Man, and what he was
Years after he had heard this heavy news.
His bodily frame had been from youth to age
Of an unusual strength. Among the rocks
He went, and still looked up to sun and cloud,
And listened to the wind; and, as before,
Performed all kinds of labour for his sheep,
And for the land, his small inheritance.
And to that hollow dell from time to time

Did he repair, to build the Fold of which
His flock had need. 'Tis not forgotten yet
The pity which was then in every heart
For the old Man – and 'tis believed by all
That many and many a day he thither went,
And never lifted up a single stone.

There, by the Sheep-fold, sometimes was he seen
Sitting alone, or with his faithful Dog,
Then old, beside him, lying at his feet.
The length of full seven years, from time to time,
He at the building of this Sheep-fold wrought,
And left the work unfinished when he died.
Three years, or little more, did Isabel
Survive her Husband: at her death the estate
Was sold, and went into a stranger's hand.
The Cottage which was named the Evening Star
Is gone – the ploughshare has been through the ground
On which it stood; great changes have been wrought
In all the neighbourhood: – yet the oak is left
That grew beside their door; and the remains
Of the unfinished Sheep-fold may be seen
Beside the boisterous brook of Green-head Ghyll.

1800

I Travelled Among Unknown Men

I travelled among unknown men,
In lands beyond the sea;
Nor, England! did I know till then
What love I bore to thee.

'Tis past, that melancholy dream!
Nor will I quit thy shore
A second time; for still I seem
To love thee more and more.

Among thy mountains did I feel
The joy of my desire;
And she I cherished turned her wheel
Beside an English fire.

Thy mornings showed, thy nights concealed
The bowers where Lucy played;
And thine too is the last green field
That Lucy's eyes surveyed.

1801

Resolution and Independence

There was a roaring in the wind all night;
The rain came heavily and fell in floods;
But now the sun is rising calm and bright;
The birds are singing in the distant woods;
Over his own sweet voice the Stock-dove broods;
The Jay makes answer as the Magpie chatters;
And all the air is filled with pleasant noise of waters.

All things that love the sun are out of doors;
The sky rejoices in the morning's birth;
The grass is bright with rain-drops; – on the moors
The hare is running races in her mirth;
And with her feet she from the plashy earth
Raises a mist; that, glittering in the sun,
Runs with her all the way, wherever she doth run.

I was a Traveller then upon the moor;
I saw the hare that raced about with joy;
I heard the woods and distant waters roar;
Or heard them not, as happy as a boy:
The pleasant season did my heart employ:

My old remembrances went from me wholly;
And all the ways of men, so vain and melancholy.

But, as it sometimes chanceth, from the might
Of joy in minds that can no further go,
As high as we have mounted in delight
In our dejection do we sink as low;
To me that morning did it happen so;
And fears and fancies thick upon me came;
Dim sadness – and blind thoughts, I knew not, nor could name.

I heard the sky-lark warbling in the sky;
And I bethought me of the playful hare:
Even such a happy Child of earth am I;
Even as these blissful creatures do I fare;
Far from the world I walk, and from all care;
But there may come another day to me—
Solitude, pain of heart, distress, and poverty.

My whole life I have lived in pleasant thought,
As if life's business were a summer mood;

As if all needful things would come unsought
To genial faith, still rich in genial good;
But how can He expect that others should
Build for him, sow for him, and at his call
Love him, who for himself will take no heed at all?

I thought of Chatterton, the marvellous Boy,
The sleepless Soul that perished in his pride;
Of Him who walked in glory and in joy
Following his plough, along the mountain-side:
By our own spirits are we deified:
We Poets in our youth begin in gladness;
But thereof come in the end despondency and madness.

Now, whether it were by peculiar grace,
A leading from above, a something given,
Yet it befel, that, in this lonely place,
When I with these untoward thoughts had striven,
Beside a pool bare to the eye of heaven
I saw a Man before me unawares:
The oldest man he seemed that ever wore grey hairs.

As a huge stone is sometimes seen to lie
Couched on the bald top of an eminence;

Wonder to all who do the same espy,

By what means it could thither come, and whence;

So that it seems a thing endued with sense:

Like a sea-beast crawled forth, that on a shelf

Of rock or sand reposeth, there to sun itself;

Such seemed this Man, not all alive nor dead,

Nor all asleep – in his extreme old age:

His body was bent double, feet and head

Coming together in life's pilgrimage;

As if some dire constraint of pain, or rage

Of sickness felt by him in times long past,

A more than human weight upon his frame had cast.

Himself he propped, limbs, body, and pale face,

Upon a long grey staff of shaven wood:

And, still as I drew near with gentle pace,

Upon the margin of that moorish flood

Motionless as a cloud the old Man stood,

That heareth not the loud winds when they call;

And moveth all together, if it move at all.

At length, himself unsettling, he the pond

Stirred with his staff, and fixedly did look

Upon the muddy water, which he conned,
As if he had been reading in a book:
And now a stranger's privilege I took;
And, drawing to his side, to him did say,
'This morning gives us promise of a glorious day.'

A gentle answer did the old Man make,
In courteous speech which forth he slowly drew:
And him with further words I thus bespake,
'What occupation do you there pursue?
This is a lonesome place for one like you.'
Ere he replied, a flash of mild surprise
Broke from the sable orbs of his yet-vivid eyes.

His words came feebly, from a feeble chest,
But each in solemn order followed each,
With something of a lofty utterance drest—
Choice word and measured phrase, above the reach
Of ordinary men; a stately speech;
Such as grave Livers do in Scotland use,
Religious men, who give to God and man their dues.

He told, that to these waters he had come
To gather leeches, being old and poor:

Employment hazardous and wearisome!
And he had many hardships to endure:
From pond to pond he roamed, from moor to moor;
Housing, with God's good help, by choice or chance;
And in this way he gained an honest maintenance.

The old Man still stood talking by my side;
But now his voice to me was like a stream
Scarce heard; nor word from word could I divide;
And the whole body of the Man did seem
Like one whom I had met with in a dream;
Or like a man from some far region sent,
To give me human strength, by apt admonishment.

My former thoughts returned: the fear that kills;
And hope that is unwilling to be fed;
Cold, pain, and labour, and all fleshly ills;
And mighty Poets in their misery dead.
—Perplexed, and longing to be comforted,
My question eagerly did I renew,
'How is it that you live, and what is it you do?'

He with a smile did then his words repeat;
And said, that, gathering leeches, far and wide

He travelled; stirring thus about his feet
The waters of the pools where they abide.
'Once I could meet with them on every side;
But they have dwindled long by slow decay;
Yet still I persevere, and find them where I may.'

While he was talking thus, the lonely place,
The old Man's shape, and speech – all troubled me:
In my mind's eye I seemed to see him pace
About the weary moors continually,
Wandering about alone and silently.
While I these thoughts within myself pursued,
He, having made a pause, the same discourse renewed.

And soon with this he other matter blended,
Cheerfully uttered, with demeanour kind,
But stately in the main; and when he ended,
I could have laughed myself to scorn to find
In that decrepit Man so firm a mind.
'God,' said I, 'be my help and stay secure;
I'll think of the Leech-gatherer on the lonely moor!'

1802

THE SOLITARY REAPER

Behold her, single in the field,
Yon solitary Highland Lass!
Reaping and singing by herself;
Stop here, or gently pass!
Alone she cuts and binds the grain,
And sings a melancholy strain;
O listen! for the Vale profound
Is overflowing with the sound.

No Nightingale did ever chaunt
More welcome notes to weary bands
Of travellers in some shady haunt,
Among Arabian sands:
A voice so thrilling ne'er was heard
In spring-time from the Cuckoo-bird,
Breaking the silence of the seas
Among the farthest Hebrides.

Will no one tell me what she sings?—
Perhaps the plaintive numbers flow
For old, unhappy, far-off things,
And battles long ago:

Or is it some more humble lay,
Familiar matter of today?
Some natural sorrow, loss, or pain,
That has been, and may be again?

Whate'er the theme, the Maiden sang
As if her song could have no ending;
I saw her singing at her work,
And o'er the sickle bending;
—I listened, motionless and still;
And, as I mounted up the hill,
The music in my heart I bore,
Long after it was heard no more.

1803–05

Elegiac Stanzas

Suggested by a Picture of Peele Castle in a Storm,
Painted by Sir George Beaumont

I was thy neighbour once, thou rugged Pile!
Four summer weeks I dwelt in sight of thee:
I saw thee every day; and all the while
Thy Form was sleeping on a glassy sea.

So pure the sky, so quiet was the air!
So like, so very like, was day to day!
Whene'er I looked, thy Image still was there;
It trembled, but it never passed away.

How perfect was the calm! it seemed no sleep;
No mood, which season takes away, or brings:
I could have fancied that the mighty Deep
Was even the gentlest of all gentle Things.

Ah! Then, if mine had been the Painter's hand,
To express what then I saw; and add the gleam,
The light that never was, on sea or land,
The consecration, and the Poet's dream;

I would have planted thee, thou hoary Pile
Amid a world how different from this!
Beside a sea that could not cease to smile;
On tranquil land, beneath a sky of bliss.

Thou shouldst have seemed a treasure-house divine
Of peaceful years; a chronicle of heaven;—
Of all the sunbeams that did ever shine
The very sweetest had to thee been given.

A Picture had it been of lasting ease,
Elysian quiet, without toil or strife;
No motion but the moving tide, a breeze,
Or merely silent Nature's breathing life.

Such, in the fond illusion of my heart,
Such Picture would I at that time have made:
And seen the soul of truth in every part,
A stedfast peace that might not be betrayed.

So once it would have been, – 'tis so no more;
I have submitted to a new control:
A power is gone, which nothing can restore;
A deep distress hath humanised my Soul.

Not for a moment could I now behold
A smiling sea, and be what I have been:
The feeling of my loss will ne'er be old;
This, which I know, I speak with mind serene.

Then, Beaumont, Friend! who would have been the Friend,
If he had lived, of Him whom I deplore,
This work of thine I blame not, but commend;
This sea in anger, and that dismal shore.

O 'tis a passionate Work! – yet wise and well,
Well chosen is the spirit that is here;
That Hulk which labours in the deadly swell,
This rueful sky, this pageantry of fear!

And this huge Castle, standing here sublime,
love to see the look with which it braves,
Cased in the unfeeling armour of old time,
The lightning, the fierce wind, and trampling waves.

Farewell, farewell the heart that lives alone,
Housed in a dream, at distance from the Kind!
Such happiness, wherever it be known,
Is to be pitied; for 'tis surely blind.

But welcome fortitude, and patient cheer,
And frequent sights of what is to be borne!
Such sights, or worse, as are before me here.—
Not without hope we suffer and we mourn.

1805

With Ships the Sea Was Sprinkled Far and Nigh

With Ships the sea was sprinkled far and nigh,
Like stars in heaven, and joyously it showed;
Some lying fast at anchor in the road,
Some veering up and down, one knew not why.
A goodly Vessel did I then espy
Come like a giant from a haven broad;
And lustily along the bay she strode,
Her tackling rich, and of apparel high.
This Ship was nought to me, nor I to her,
Yet I pursued her with a Lover's look;
This Ship to all the rest did I prefer:
When will she turn, and whither? She will brook
No tarrying; where She comes the winds must stir:
On went She, and due north her journey took.

1806

Surprised by Joy – Impatient as the Wind

Surprised by joy – impatient as the Wind
I turned to share the transport – Oh! with whom
But Thee, deep buried in the silent tomb,
That spot which no vicissitude can find?

Love, faithful love, recalled thee to my mind—
But how could I forget thee? Through what power,
Even for the least division of an hour,
Have I been so beguiled as to be blind
To my most grievous loss? – That thought's return

Was the worst pang that sorrow ever bore,
Save one, one only, when I stood forlorn,
Knowing my heart's best treasure was no more;
That neither present time, nor years unborn
Could to my sight that heavenly face restore.

1813–14

Extempore Effusion upon the Death of James Hogg

When first, descending from the moorlands,
I saw the Stream of Yarrow glide
Along a bare and open valley,
The Ettrick Shepherd was my guide.
When last along its banks I wandered,

Through groves that had begun to shed
Their golden leaves upon the pathways,
My steps the Border-minstrel led.
The mighty Minstrel breathes no longer,
'Mid mouldering ruins low he lies;

And death upon the braes of Yarrow,
Has closed the Shepherd-poet's eyes:
Nor has the rolling year twice measured,
From sign to sign, its stedfast course,
Since every mortal power of Coleridge

Was frozen at its marvellous source;
The rapt One, of the godlike forehead,
The heaven-eyed creature sleeps in earth:

And Lamb, the frolic and the gentle,
Has vanished from his lonely hearth.

Like clouds that rake the mountain-summits,
Or waves that own no curbing hand,
How fast has brother followed brother,
From sunshine to the sunless land!
Yet I, whose lids from infant slumber

Were earlier raised, remain to hear
A timid voice, that asks in whispers,
'Who next will drop and disappear?'
Our haughty life is crowned with darkness,
Like London with its own black wreath,

On which with thee, O Crabbe! forth-looking,
I gazed from Hampstead's breezy heath.
As if but yesterday departed,
Thou too art gone before; but why,
O'er ripe fruit, seasonably gathered,

Should frail survivors heave a sigh?
Mourn rather for that holy Spirit,

Sweet as the spring, as ocean deep;

For Her who, ere her summer faded,

Has sunk into a breathless sleep.

No more of old romantic sorrows,

For slaughtered Youth or love-lorn Maid!

With sharper grief is Yarrow smitten,

And Ettrick mourns with her their Poet dead.

1835

SOCIETY

&

DAILY LIFE

To My Sister

It is the first mild day of March:
Each minute sweeter than before
The redbreast sings from the tall larch
That stands beside our door.

There is a blessing in the air,
Which seems a sense of joy to yield
To the bare trees, and mountains bare,
And grass in the green field.

My sister! ('tis a wish of mine)
Now that our morning meal is done,
Make haste, your morning task resign;
Come forth and feel the sun.

Edward will come with you; – and, pray,
Put on with speed your woodland dress;
And bring no book: for this one day
We'll give to idleness.

No joyless forms shall regulate
Our living calendar:
We from today, my Friend, will date
The opening of the year.

Love, now a universal birth,
From heart to heart is stealing,
From earth to man, from man to earth:
—It is the hour of feeling.

One moment now may give us more
Than years of toiling reason:
Our minds shall drink at every pore
The spirit of the season.

Some silent laws our hearts will make,
Which they shall long obey:
We for the year to come may take
Our temper from today.

And from the blessed power that rolls
About, below, above,
We'll frame the measure of our souls:
They shall be tuned to love.

Then come, my Sister! come, I pray,
With speed put on your woodland dress;
And bring no book: for this one day
We'll give to idleness.

1798

A Character

I marvel how Nature could ever find space
For so many strange contrasts in one human face:
There's thought and no thought, and there's paleness and bloom
And bustle and sluggishness, pleasure and gloom.

There's weakness, and strength both redundant and vain;
Such strength as, if ever affliction and pain
Could pierce through a temper that's soft to disease,
Would be rational peace – a philosopher's ease.

There's indifference, alike when he fails or succeeds,
And attention full ten times as much as there needs;
Pride where there's no envy, there's so much of joy;
And mildness, and spirit both forward and coy.

There's freedom, and sometimes a diffident stare
Of shame scarcely seeming to know that she's there,
There's virtue, the title it surely may claim,
Yet wants heaven knows what to be worthy the name.

This picture from nature may seem to depart,
Yet the Man would at once run away with your heart;
And I for five centuries right gladly would be
Such an odd such a kind happy creature as he.

1800

WRITTEN IN MARCH

While Resting on the Bridge
at the Foot of Brother's Water

The Cock is crowing,
The stream is flowing,
The small birds twitter,
The lake doth glitter,
The green field sleeps in the sun;
The oldest and youngest
Are at work with the strongest;
The cattle are grazing,
Their heads never raising;
There are forty feeding like one!

Like an army defeated
The snow hath retreated,
And now doth fare ill
On the top of the bare hill;
The Ploughboy is whooping – anon – anon:
There's joy in the mountains;
There's life in the fountains;
Small clouds are sailing,
Blue sky prevailing;
The rain is over and gone!

1802

The Sun Has Long Been Set

The sun has long been set,
The stars are out by twos and threes,
The little birds are piping yet
Among the bushes and trees;
There's a cuckoo, and one or two thrushes,
And a far-off wind that rushes,
And a sound of water that gushes,
And the cuckoo's sovereign cry
Fills all the hollow of the sky.

Who would go 'parading'
In London, 'and masquerading',
On such a night of June
With that beautiful soft half-moon,
And all these innocent blisses?
On such a night as this is!

1802

London, 1802

Milton! thou should'st be living at this hour:
England hath need of thee: she is a fen
Of stagnant waters: altar, sword, and pen,
Fireside, the heroic wealth of hall and bower,
Have forfeited their ancient English dower
Of inward happiness. We are selfish men;
Oh! raise us up, return to us again;
And give us manners, virtue, freedom, power.
Thy soul was like a Star, and dwelt apart:
Thou hadst a voice whose sound was like the sea:
Pure as the naked heavens, majestic, free,
So didst thou travel on life's common way,
In cheerful godliness; and yet thy heart
The lowliest duties on herself did lay.

1802

The Kitten and Falling Leaves

That way look, my Infant, lo!
What a pretty baby-show!
See the Kitten on the wall,
Sporting with the leaves that fall,
Withered leaves – one – two – and three—
From the lofty elder-tree!
Through the calm and frosty air
Of this morning bright and fair,
Eddying round and round they sink
Softly, slowly: one might think,
From the motions that are made,
Every little leaf conveyed
Sylph or Faery hither tending,
—To this lower world descending,
Each invisible and mute,
In his wavering parachute.

—But the Kitten, how she starts,
Crouches, stretches, paws, and darts!
First at one, and then its fellow
Just as light and just as yellow;

There are many now – now one—
Now they stop and there are none:
What intenseness of desire
In her upward eye of fire!
With a tiger-leap half-way
Now she meets the coming prey,
Lets it go as fast, and then
Has it in her power again:
Now she works with three or four,
Like an Indian conjurer;
Quick as he in feats of art,
Far beyond in joy of heart.
Were her antics played in the eye
Of a thousand standers-by,
Clapping hands with shout and stare,
What would little Tabby care
For the plaudits of the crowd?
Over happy to be proud,
Over wealthy in the treasure
Of her own exceeding pleasure!

'Tis a pretty baby-treat;
Nor, I deem, for me unmeet;
Here, for neither Babe nor me,
Other play-mate can I see.
Of the countless living things,
That with stir of feet and wings
(In the sun or under shade,
Upon bough or grassy blade)
And with busy revellings,
Chirp and song, and murmurings,
Made this orchard's narrow space,
And this vale so blithe a place;
Multitudes are swept away
Never more to breathe the day:
Some are sleeping; some in bands
Travelled into distant lands;
Others slunk to moor and wood,
Far from human neighbourhood;
And, among the Kinds that keep
With us closer fellowship,
With us openly abide,
All have laid their mirth aside.

Where is he that giddy Sprite,
Blue-cap, with his colours bright,
Who was blest as bird could be,
Feeding in the apple-tree;
Made such wanton spoil and rout,
Turning blossoms inside out;
Hung – head pointing towards the ground—
Fluttered, perched, into a round
Bound himself, and then unbound;
Lithest, gaudiest Harlequin!
Prettiest tumbler ever seen!
Light of heart and light of limb;
What is now become of Him?
Lambs, that through the mountains went
Frisking, bleating merriment,
When the year was in its prime,
They are sobered by this time.
If you look to vale or hill,
If you listen, all is still,
Save a little neighbouring rill,
That from out the rocky ground
Strikes a solitary sound.
Vainly glitter hill and plain,

And the air is calm in vain;
Vainly Morning spreads the lure
Of a sky serene and pure;
Creature none can she decoy
Into open sign of joy:
Is it that they have a fear
Of the dreary season near?
Or that other pleasures be
Sweeter even than gaiety?

Yet, whate'er enjoyments dwell
In the impenetrable cell
Of the silent heart which Nature
Furnishes to every creature;
Whatsoe'er we feel and know
Too sedate for outward show,
Such a light of gladness breaks,
Pretty Kitten! from thy freaks,
—Spreads with such a living grace
O'er my little Dora's face;
Yes, the sight so stirs and charms
Thee, Baby, laughing in my arms,
That almost I could repine

That your transports are not mine,
That I do not wholly fare
Even as ye do, thoughtless pair!
And I will have my careless season
Spite of melancholy reason,
Will walk through life in such a way
That, when time brings on decay,
Now and then I may possess
Hours of perfect gladsomeness.
—Pleased by any random toy;
By a kitten's busy joy,
Or an infant's laughing eye
Sharing in the ecstasy;
I would fare like that or this,
Find my wisdom in my bliss;
Keep the sprightly soul awake,
And have faculties to take,
Even from things by sorrow wrought,
Matter for a jocund thought,
Spite of care, and spite of grief,
To gambol with Life's falling Leaf.

1804

THE WORLD IS TOO MUCH WITH US; LATE AND SOON

The world is too much with us; late and soon,
Getting and spending, we lay waste our powers:
Little we see in Nature that is ours;
We have given our hearts away, a sordid boon!
This Sea that bares her bosom to the moon;
The winds that will be howling at all hours,
And are up-gathered now like sleeping flowers;
For this, for every thing, we are out of tune;
It moves us not. – Great God! I'd rather be
A Pagan suckled in a creed outworn;
So might I, standing on this pleasant lea,
Have glimpses that would make me less forlorn;
Have sight of Proteus rising from the sea;
Or hear old Triton blow his wreathed horn.

1806

SONG FOR THE SPINNING WHEEL

Swiftly turn the murmuring wheel!
Night has brought the welcome hour,
When the weary fingers feel
Help, as if from faery power;
Dewy night o'ershades the ground;
Turn the swift wheel round and round!

Now, beneath the starry sky,
Couch the widely-scattered sheep;
—Ply the pleasant labour, ply!
For the spindle, while they sleep,
Runs with speed more smooth and fine,
Gathering up a trustier line.

Short-lived likings may be bred
By a glance from fickle eyes;
But true love is like the thread
Which the kindly wool supplies,
When the flocks are all at rest
Sleeping on the mountain's breast.

1812

WHEN HAUGHTY EXPECTATIONS PROSTRATE LIE

When haughty expectations prostrate lie,
And grandeur crouches like a guilty thing,
Oft shall the lowly weak, till nature bring
Mature release, in fair society
Survive, and Fortune's utmost anger try;
Like these frail snow-drops that together cling,
And nod their helmets, smitten by the wing
Of many a furious whirl-blast sweeping by.
Observe the faithful flowers! if small to great
May lead the thoughts, thus struggling used to stand
The Emathian phalanx, nobly obstinate;
And so the bright immortal Theban band,
Whom onset, fiercely urged at Jove's command,
Might overwhelm, but could not separate!

1819

MUTABILITY

From low to high doth dissolution climb,
And sink from high to low, along a scale
Of awful notes, whose concord shall not fail;
A musical but melancholy chime,
Which they can hear who meddle not with crime,
Nor avarice, nor over-anxious care.
Truth fails not; but her outward forms that bear
The longest date do melt like frosty rime,
That in the morning whitened hill and plain
And is no more; drop like the tower sublime
Of yesterday, which royally did wear
His crown of weeds, but could not even sustain
Some casual shout that broke the silent air,
Or the unimaginable touch of Time.

1821

CALM IS THE FRAGRANT AIR AND LOTH TO LOSE

Calm is the fragrant air, and loth to lose
Day's grateful warmth, tho' moist with falling dews.
Look for the stars, you'll say that there are none;
Look up a second time, and, one by one,
You mark them twinkling out with silvery light,
And wonder how they could elude the sight!
The birds, of late so noisy in their bowers,
Warbled a while with faint and fainter powers,
But now are silent as the dim-seen flowers:
Nor does the village Church-clock's iron tone
The time's and season's influence disown;
Nine beats distinctly to each other bound
In drowsy sequence – how unlike the sound
That, in rough winter, oft inflicts a fear
On fireside listeners, doubting what they hear!
The shepherd, bent on rising with the sun,
Had closed his door before the day was done,
And now with thankful heart to bed doth creep,
And joins his little children in their sleep.
The bat, lured forth where trees the lane o'ershade,

Flits and reflits along the close arcade;
The busy dorhawk chases the white moth
With burring note, which Industry and Sloth
Might both be pleased with, for it suits them both.
A stream is heard – I see it not, but know
By its soft music whence the waters flow:
Wheels and the tread of hoofs are heard no more;
One boat there was, but it will touch the shore
With the next dipping of its slackened oar;
Faint sound, that, for the gayest of the gay,
Might give to serious thought a moment's sway,
As a last token of man's toilsome day!

1832

MOST SWEET IT IS WITH UNUPLIFTED EYES

Most sweet it is with unuplifted eyes
To pace the ground, if path be there or none,
While a fair region round the traveller lies
Which he forbears again to look upon;
Pleased rather with some soft ideal scene,
The work of Fancy, or some happy tone
Of meditation, slipping in between
The beauty coming and the beauty gone.
If Thought and Love desert us, from that day
Let us break off all commerce with the Muse:
With Thought and Love companions of our way,
Whate'er the senses take or may refuse,
The Mind's internal heaven shall shed her dews
Of inspiration on the humblest lay.

1833

A Night Thought

Lo! where the Moon along the sky
Sails with her happy destiny;
Oft is she hid from mortal eye
Or dimly seen,
But when the clouds asunder fly
How bright her mien!
Far different we – a froward race,
Thousands though rich in Fortune's grace
With cherished sullenness of pace
Their way pursue,
Ingrates who wear a smileless face
The whole year through.
If kindred humours e'er would make
My spirit droop for drooping's sake,
From Fancy following in thy wake,
Bright ship of heaven!
A counter impulse let me take
And be forgiven.

1837

INDEX

A

'A Character' (1800) 138

'A Night Piece' (1798) 16

'A Night Thought' (1837) 157

'A Slumber Did My Spirit Seal' (1799) 97

'A Whirl-blast from Behind the Hill' (1798) 18

'An Evening Walk' (extracts) (1787–89) 11

'Anecdote for Fathers' (1798) 56

'Animal Tranquillity and Decay' (1797) 90

C

'Calm Is All Nature as a Resting Wheel' (c. 1786) 89

'Calm Is the Fragrant Air and Loth to Lose' (1832) 154

'Composed upon Westminster Bridge, September 3, 1802' (1802) 43

E

'Elegiac Stanzas, Suggested by a Picture of Peele Castle in a Storm, Painted by Sir George Beaumont' (1805) 125

'Expostulation and Reply' (1798) 22

'Extempore Effusion upon the Death of James Hogg' (1835) 131

F

'Fairest, Brightest Hues of Ether Fade, The' (published 1815) 50

'Fountain, The' (1799) 68

H

'Hart-Leap Well' (1800) 26

I

'I Travelled Among Unknown Men' (1801) 115

'I Wandered Lonely as a Cloud' (1804) 84

'It Is a Beauteous Evening, Calm and Free' (1802) 42

'It Was an April Morning: Fresh and Clear' (c. 1800) 36

K

'Kitten and Falling Leaves, The' (1804) 144

L

'Lines Written in Early Spring' (1798) 20

'Lines, Composed a Few Miles Above Tintern Abbey' (1798) 60

'London, 1802' (1802) 143

'Lucy Gray; or, Solitude' (1799) 101

M

'Matthew' (1799) 95

'Michael' (extract) (1800) 108

'Most Sweet It Is with Unuplifted Eyes' (1833) 156

'Mutability' (1821) 153

'My Heart Leaps up when I Behold' (1802) 41

O

'Ode: Intimations of Immortality from Recollections of Early Childhood' (1803–06) 74

'Oh Nightingale, Thou Surely Art' (1807) 48

'On Nature's Invitation Do I Come' (c. 1800) 39

P

'Prelude, The' (Book I) (extract) (1798–1839) 53

R

'Resolution and Independence' (1802) 116

S

'She Dwelt Among the Untrodden Ways' (1799) 98

'She Was a Phantom of Delight' (1804) 44

'Solitary Reaper, The' (1803–05) 123

'Song for the Spinning Wheel' (1812) 151

'Sparrow's Nest, The' (1801) 72

'Stars Are Mansions Built by Nature's Hand, The' (1820) 51

'Strange Fits of Passion Have I Known' (1799) 99

'Sun Has Long Been Set, The' (1802) 142

'Surprised by Joy – Impatient as the Wind' (1813–14) 130

T

'Tables Turned, The' (1798) 24

'There Is a Little Unpretending Rill' (c. 1806) 86

'Three Years She Grew in Sun and Shower' (1799) 105

'To a Butterfly' (1802) 73

'To a Sky-Lark' (1805) 46

'To My Sister' (1798) 135

'To the Cuckoo' (1827) 87

W

'We Are Seven' (1798) 91

'When Haughty Expectations Prostrate Lie' (1819) 152

'With Ships the Sea Was Sprinkled Far and Nigh' (1806) 129

'World Is Too Much with Us; Late and Soon, The' (1806) 150

'Written in March' (1802) 140